Feeding
The
Monster

(some) other books by EMP

Bury My Heart In The Gutter
by Dan Denton

Those Who Favor Fire, Those Who Pray To Fire
by Ben Brindise & Justin Karcher

Ginger Roots Are Best Taken Orally
by Tom Farris & Victor Clevenger

This One's For Me
by Ellen Lutnick

What We Face Walking Out The Front Door
by Zophia McDougal

The Former Lives of Saints
by Ezhno Martin & Damian Rucci

Don't Lose Your Head
by Jeanette Powers

Beautiful Earthworms & Abominable Stars
by Ezhno Martin & Jeanette Powers

Feeding
The
Monster

Poems by

Adrian Lime &
Michael Grover

EMP
Toledo, Ohio
http://www.empbooks.com

Copyright © 2018 Adrian Lime & Michael Grover

We find discussions of our rights - as publishers and authors - to be laughable, all things considered. Please claim this work as your own. Please republish it and sell it on street corners. Please include our material in ALL of your get-rich-quick schemes. All we ask is that you accept responsibility for any libel lawsuits. Speaking of which ... This book is a complete work of fiction. Names, characters, places, opinions, dreams, dates, impressions, monologues about a certain New York City basketball team, emotional trauma, statistics, and predictions are products of the author's imagination and/or are symptoms of mental illness. We are not in the business of accepting responsibility for anything and will deny we actually made this book and blame Jokim Noah at every turn.

First Edition

ISBN: 978-0-9997138-3-9
LOC: 2018963399
10 19 33 34 6 11 1973

Design, Layout, and Edits: Ezhno Martín
Cover Design and Painting: Craig Firsdon
Interior Photos/Drawings: Creative Commons (the internet)

TOC

preface

by Adrian Lime // pg i

dying where no one would hear
my last whispering

by Michael Grover // pg 1

unsolicited advice for a new
factory worker

by Adrian Lime // pg 19

This book was made in a factory.

This physical book you hold in your hand was made in a factory. Mostly by machines. No letterpress printing on artisan paper folded and hand-sewn and personal. No— this book was printed by machines— collated, glued, and bound by other machines— spat out onto a conveyor and slid to the end of some line in some factory somewhere, fast, efficient and cost-effective.

But consider that in some warehouse in—I don't know, Cincinnati—there's a forklift operator loading 2-ton pallets of paper with his hi-low into the back of a semi-trailer, just trying to get through his shift so he can get to the bar and drink away the knowledge that his grown kids still hate him because he drinks too much. There is a shadow of that man in this book.

At the end of the line where these new books are printed and bound, there is a woman waiting— gathering up the books and stacking them in boxes. Stack it, pack it, tape it shut, slap a label on the side and slide it down the line. Her hands know the work so well, her mind drifts— she's working out the math of how to keep the electric on and still afford school clothes for her kids. Her supervisor keeps staring at her, her car needs a muffler, and she's out of fucking cigarettes. The book in your hand has heard her dreaming.

Load the boxes onto more pallets, bills of lade wrapped into plastic, pallet-jacked onto another semi, and then off they go to the publisher. It's late, and the trucker is impatient. He's got twelve more loads to run and he's getting paid the same even if it takes all night. He wants to get moving. While he waits, he checks his phone hoping not to find a text from his dispatcher. He reads a message from his wife— she's gotten into Southern Illinois on a full scholarship. Some of the pride and relief of that trucker— and some from his wife— has sunk deep into these pages.

Most of the poems in this book were written in a factory— scribbled onto slips of paper and tucked into sweaty pockets at odd moments, or poked into a note on a phone to be emailed to ourselves for when the shift ends and we can have a moment when the machines aren't ganging up on us. But it's important to remember that in this book are the dreams and sadnesses, the fears and fantasies, the busted knuckles and tired feet of all the many people whose hands transported this book into yours.

Including the poets.

Michael Grover

dying where no one would hear
my last whispering

the machines waited for me

-1-

The machines waited for me — Antler

The dirt never washes off
even if I wash it off
I could never wash it all off
anyway, it'll come back the next day
& I will wash it off again
but I never get it all

maybe there's some in my beard
inside my nose
caked under my nails

That thick black dirt
that consumes everything
in the factory
the machines spit it out
it is the air you breathe
unless you prefer
to fog up your safety goggles
with a dust mask
The dirt never washes off
even if I wash it off
my bathwater a murky gray
a ring around the tub

Factory Black

-2-

For the totem pole of my personality to be carved — Antler

They are all men that work in the factory
I've heard a few men
including my work partner Kevin say
There's no woman that can do this
I agree with them
but for different reasons
There is one woman that comes in
she cleans the front hallway,
the break room and the bosses office upstairs
where they watch us on camera
like prison guards
where men lose their souls
thinkin' their savin' their own

My work partner Kevin yells things at her
as she cleans by the front door
he gets all excited
and tells me how he loves her titties

she moves around nervously
like she did something wrong

-3-

The noise of the miraculous machines of the factory — Antler

Overtime is mandatory
for the temps in the factory
last week we started working saturdays
which is a brutal unpleasant day
we gotta be there a little before five am
but the check is nice

This week they put up the notice
on wednesday that the plant
would be running on saturday

I put in a request for the day off
I had scheduled a Poetry performance
I just wrote down performance

After lunch the supervisor comes up
So Michael what kind of performance is this
I said, *It's Poetry ...*
like spoken word stuff

He started laughing hysterically

-4-

I relished the words I would write — Antler

(Two Days Before The Fourth Of July)

Thank you america
for three-day-weekends
three days to recover
from the factory grind
from the sinus infection
from breathing the air
thank you america
let the birthday party begin

-5-

Dying where no one would hear my last whispering — Antler

there is no Poetry in the factory
well...
Poetry lives there
don't get me wrong
I sneak it out in my head
there is Poetry in the noise of the machines
it all blends into static

There is no Poetry in the factory
I am mocked for being a Poet
as a co-worker and I
walk back from lunch
where he showed me his Poetry in private
in a different parking lot

-6-

As multitudes worked on machines I would work on — Antler

Today the wire line was a revolving door
Larry left at nine-thirty
for a doctors appointment
he showed up for at one-thirty
he just didn't want to get
chewed up & spit out
by the machine today
same as everyday
he just didn't want to feel
like death walking

some days I loathe Larry's laziness
some days I envy his freedom

Then they sent Big Tim
the forklift operator
the large angry ex-professional wrestler
Big Tim did not enjoy working the wire line
he wore his heart on his sleeve
covered in tattoos

Big Tim only worked the wire line until lunch
Then came Matt
who worked his own line in the back

Matt hates the wire line
Matt hates his own line

Matt knows they just run them all too hard
to suck every dollar out of them
but he stuck it out for the rest of the day

Brian the operator came down
and picked with us
he yelled at me
for letting too much shit through
it wasn't that I was letting
too much shit through
it was that he was running
too much shit

The supervisor Eric also came to pick with us
He would tell me
Come on Michael
You're not gonna pay the rent
staying home writing Poetry

I told him
he would never be
a motivational speaker

-7-

Who will remember the Continental Can Company — Antler

Coughs are what remain
of the factory when you are home
black chunks of mucus
that you cough up
black shit that cakes
inside of your nose
that is the factory
following us home
like a ghost
soaked in your dirty clothes & sweat
that is the factory
following us home

-8-

Or what they'd think of this poem — Antler

Us workers of the factory
the one place we see each other
when we're off the clock
is in & out of the liquor store
or drinking at some bar

these are the points
that we intersect

−9−

I see my shadow working on the shadow of a machine. — Antler

I will never fit my father's boots
too big
I fit my own boots just fine
I walk through life

I will never fit my father's boots
too big
my father sent a box
of his old winter work gear
he doesn't need it
being retired in Florida
I told him I would find a home
for what did not fit
and there they were
those big insulated boots
too big

-10-

To them the prostitutes must be beautiful — Antler

It's easy to die
after leaving the factory
to turn everything off
& be reborn

-11-

*And for suicide to long for me as the years ran
into the mirror* — Antler

Big Kev tells me
how the plant manager
said he was going to fire me
last month when I left early
to go read Poetry in Indiana
I told them I was going to visit friends
but word travels fast in the factory

-12-

Show me the pageant of every creature — Antler

When your body is so beat up
that it is useless
there is only recovery
this is the way they want us
pushed to the limit
anyone that's been here
for any amount of time
will tell you that

they will tell you
how this plant will grind you down
they will tell you
how brutal the winter is
& we're only just starting to feel a chill

-13-

How America uses 115 million cans each day — Antler

Matt's worked in the factory for five years
one of the veterans
hell of a nice guy
talks to everyone
veterans to new hires
can talk about sports forever
Matt hates the plant as much as anyone there does

If you work with him you will see him
stressed out, literally foaming at the mouth
I tell him he shouldn't sweat it so much
Matt went to the doctor
he's been having trouble breathing
doctor says it could be lung cancer
now Matt is scared
he and two other veterans
start wearing dust masks every day
too little, too late

-14-

Millions of humans enter factories at dawn
How many have their arms raised to the sun? — Antler

Good morning Toledo
that eternal flame of optimism
bright murals catchy slogans
optimism as thick as the air is polluted
pollution from factories full
of hard-assed workers
that would explode
if only they could afford to

Hours cut
dignity stripped
so much rage
contained in those aluminum walls

someday the factory will close
the owners really won't be affected
the workers will carry
their broken bodies away
& survive

Adrian Lime

unsolicited advice for a new
factory worker

I get ten seconds
between each car
so I write haiku
all night long

Adjustments

At the plant today,
from across the commissary, I saw
Becky Lautner *(that's not her real name)*
hook her two rough thumbs
through the fabric of her Iron Maiden t-shirt
into some recess of her brassiere,
and with a slight wince and a sort of
swooping grace hoist her two, frankly massive
breasts into a more comfortable, or let's say less
uncomfortable position.
                     And if that's not already
enough to spark notice, she then
heaved out such a cathartic sigh of relief
that even I felt it from all the way across
that field of laminate tables and Bakelite
lunch trays, and it made me instantly, and
hopefully forgivably, feel a little guilty
for complaining about my aching feet.

Unsolicited Advice for
a New Factory Worker

This is what you do.
You get up very early.
You go in.
You get your station ready
and you start working.

You get shit on by bosses
and backed up by brothers.
You bust knuckles, and earn your pay.
It's a mess, but you go through it together.

You take your breaks and drink water.
You stretch your back
and think about your wife.
You do your job and try to daydream.
Some days are fine, some days
you don't talk about.
Then you go home, eat a little something,
cramp up and go to bed.
Start again the next day.

Fit your writing in here and there,
and here again.
And there again.

Some time to breathe a little,
some time for your family,

... the honest-to-Christ only reason
you force yourself through it all.
Then there's that moment
to recognize that it could be worse
and it could be better.
But it could be worse.
But we can make it better.

And tomorrow
you go back into that sweaty bitch
and do it again.

That's what you do.

how to avoid having
your fingers torn off

no more thoughts except those
that pass the time on the line
to dissolve poof as jokes —
this humor
this skiff of trite fun
these are thoughts
dedicated to knees that distend
fingers that dissolve into hands.
impact wrench with all torque
and no smarts.
if the safety's off
for fuck sake take off your gloves.
no more thoughts on the line
except those that pass time
and keep you three mils from insanity,
three mils from the emergency room.
this is not poof as a joke.
it is the sad humor
a mind grabs at when all at once
it's left to consider desperate protection
and mindless boredom.

Gap in the Line!

Gap in the line!
Gap in the line!

Everybody quick!
Scurry to your phones!
We may only have seconds!
Check your Facebooks and Twitters.
Gap in the line, fellas!

You!
Poor guy with the flip phone
scurry to your cellophane sleeve
of butter crackers tucked amongst
the crate full of gaskets — now is your moment!
Drink your water and
Lick your lips!

Gap in the line!
Looks like a big one!

Old timers!
Shamble to your fold-out chairs
and Igloo coolers.
Take a nip off that tit
and tuck it back away.
Scan the line for another old timer …
… knowingly nod, and
check your smokes.

There's a gap in the line!
Could start up any second!

You! Douchebag greasy muscle bound
twentysomething.
Now's your time to make your move!
Peacock yourself
to the cute girls, next line over ...
here's your chance!
You know they watch you
as you hoist and rivet.

Gap in the line!
It's the blue light special!
Could break anytime!

You, especially,
18-year-old legacy boy.
You get it hardest.
Stretch your shoulders now
and flex your knees.
Pump your hands to prepare
for what's coming.
Tape up your fingers and make your
Papa proud.

Assembly Line Haiku

I get 10 seconds
between each car, so I write
haiku all night long.

> Your knuckles will heal.
> Hot showers will ease your back.
> Corn Huskers Lotion.

Even when you ask
nicely, *May I have more time?*
the line keeps moving.

> Stuck watching the clock.
> You wait an hour, check again—
> five minutes have passed.

8-foot fence surrounds
the plant, armed guards patrol, and
barbed wire facing in.

> Sleeping after work
> is a race between sunrise
> and tomorrow's shift

End of third-shift bell
Steam from our necks rising like
steam from Jeep smokestacks

> On my mind, my wife
> and children. On my fingers,
> callus and grease stains.

Big, bearded hulk-man
on the line next to mine, loves
Pablo Neruda.

> Other big, bearded
> hulk-man one line down from me
> loves Charles Bukowski.

Vending machines here
sell candy, caffeine drinks, and
pain medication.

> By the fifth hour your
> back is breaking. By the tenth,
> you don't even care.

There's only so much
a fan can do, blowing this
hot factory air.

                              Line is chugging fast—
                              Charlie ate Metamucil,
                         now we wait and watch

If you hurry so
you don't fall behind, they just
add another job.

Night-Shift Factory

I'm working and plugging along, as usual
my fingertips slivered ever so slightly—
callus tabs curl like old barn paint, exposing
that which it was meant to protect.

Because we're manly men who grunt *Uuggg*
we compare scars,
and try to out-story each other,
equal parts hyperbole and horse shit—
the skin twisted off just here,
a lumpy purple bruise there,
pinkie finger splintered and healed crooked.

Vincent the mechanic is younger than me
with hands like a subway map.
He is the king of us all.
Creases so deep they swallow lifelines,
obliterate love lines, make palm-readers
blush. Vincent did not earn his calluses
by patting himself on the back.

Too many scars to count, he is a marvel.
He points to a nub absent a finger,
Never get that caught in a belt again.
Vincent is smiling.
He is always smiling.
If he doesn't have a flashlight bitten
between his teeth, seeking out
a defect, he is smiling.

Vincent points at my arm and says
You sprang a leak.
A lust red line of blood runs down
thinning itself through sweat, working
its way through arm hairs toward the hard
Spanish oak of the plywood skillets
running beneath us, as we ride along.

Thanks, I say.
I patch my arm with a sandwich napkin
and athletic tape.

It's not a sign of toughness
I didn't know I'd cut myself
on a sheared-off stud.
This is proof that the pain of factory work
is so thrumming and constant
it can make you almost pain-free.
Unburdened by specifics.
It's not that nothing hurts,
it's that everything hurts.
One more bruise
is the fourth violin in a symphony.

Like the hum and roar of machinery
and air handling all around, the burr
of the whole floor dragged beneath you
by massive screw gears,
monster teeth chewing
at steel before you, beneath you, above you,
vehicles clanging together overhead, drawn by
arm-thick chains and sprockets—

the endless bark of bosses,
the shout for stock running low,
alarms that tell us so many things at once
they don't tell us anything at all.
The clank and crash so cacophonous
and constant that the brain resets
and makes this noise
the new normal, car by car, hour by hour,
year by year,
until the sudden hush of
early morning shift-end solitude outside
is so discomfiting you secretly hope
a train stops you on your way home.
Just for the blare. The hair-of-the-dog of noise.
Just to let your ears come back slowly
like a deep-sea diver in a decompression tank.

But the deepest scars aren't in the skin.
And can't be compared with forearms, but
with stories told in heaves and laughs,
sometimes told so very quietly,
over shots and beers.
The deepest scars are in recounting
that your kids have grown four more years,
or twelve more years, or they've moved out
and left for good, and you've worked so much
you hardly knew it.
These are the scars we don't compare.

At end of shift — Vincent's working a twelve,
you're out from a ten, he shouts to me
above a fat steel swing arm,
Don't forget to change your tampon, Ginger!

Vincent is smiling.

The sandwich napkin is half-healed
into my skin and I swipe my card at the gate
to leave that factory behind me.
I don't think of it for a second when I'm home.

I hope my wife will be up when I get there.
She'll have sleep in her eyes, bed-hair,
and we'll share some coffee before
she goes to work, and I go to sleep.

Breakthrough

In my work, my gloves wear through,
revealing skin, knuckles, fingernails
worn tough by this regular grind.
Always the first to break through
is my wedding ring, which looks
at first sight, like
a golden worm,
cresting the surface
of rich garden earth after a rain,

or the first streak of morning
cracking the darkness of night.

This comforts me while I work,
when the drear overtakes the mind,
any thought you've once had blanches
and that old stiffness rises and plateaus
and fingers shudder and want to quit
and callus (mercifully achieved) splits,
opening a seam of deep pink,
the rebirth of pain once overcome.

Seeing the ring, I remember why I work —
the ring not being my wife, herself
(my wife much more brilliant, though
just as scuffed from work of her own)
but something to keep with me, to catch
my eye at an odd glance with a glimmer,
to elicit a smile I forgot I had.

I'm not worried about my wedding ring
getting scuffed up, not really,
this soft metal with the steel that abrades it—
after all the ring is just a ring.
And what it signifies,
what it proves day in day out
is much, much stronger than steel.

Originally published in Red Fez
Issue #100
May 2017
https://www.redfez.net/issue100

Career Goal

I know that retirement is not an option.
I know that there will be no pension.
I know that one day I will die
in this plant. I just hope
I don't die at the end
of my shift.

Poem Written During an Unexpected Line Break

line break holy shit finally time
to write some of these thoughts down
but what to write I've been thinking
hard all day there's got to be something
come on this won't last long
I can't believe nothing is coming
to mind there's got to be something
what the fuck the line could go
any second and I'm blank oh no
why is this happening I'm squandering
my time what am I doing with my life
just write something anything
there's so much to say
and now's the only time I've got
shit the line is starting again
motherfucker
goddam

While Leaving Work
after a Ten-Hour Overtime Shift
at the Toledo Jeep Plant on a Saturday

Hey, fuck you Adrian.

Oh yeah? Well fuck you too.

See you Monday.

See you Monday.

www.ingramcontent.com/pod-product-compliance
Lightning Source LLC
Chambersburg PA
CBHW030459010526
44118CB00011B/1005